Teddy Roosevelt

ROUGH RIDER

Teddy Roosevelt

ROUGH RIDER

by Louis Sabin
illustrated by Robert Baxter

Troll Associates

Library of Congress Cataloging in Publication Data

Sabin, Louis.
    Teddy Roosevelt, Rough Rider.

    Summary: A biography of Theodore Roosevelt, who at
the age of forty-two was the youngest man to become
President of the United States.
    1. Roosevelt, Theodore, 1858-1919—Juvenile
literature.   2. Presidents—United States—Biography—
Juvenile literature.   [1. Roosevelt, Theodore,
1858-1919.   2. Presidents]   I. Baxter, Robert,
1930-   , ill.   II. Title.
E757.S18   1986   973.91 '1 '0924 [B] [92]   85-1090
ISBN 0-8167-0555-0 (lib. bdg.)
ISBN 0-8167-0556-9 (pbk.)

Teddy Roosevelt

ROUGH RIDER

We are face to face with our destiny and we must meet it with a high and resolute courage.

The first Roosevelt came to America in 1649 and settled on Manhattan Island. He was a farmer with little money, but he had a reputation as an honest, hard-working person. With each new generation of Roosevelts, the family fortunes grew. Still, the sense of honor and responsibility to others never changed. It was into this long tradition that Theodore Roosevelt was born, on October 27, 1858. He was a member of the seventh generation of Roosevelts born in Manhattan.

Teddy was the second child of Theodore, Sr., and Martha Bulloch Roosevelt. The family, which also included three-year-old Anna, lived in a comfortable house with many servants. Mr. Roosevelt and his four brothers were successful in banking, real estate, and business. They all lived within a few blocks of one another, and their families were very close. For the Roosevelt children there were always cousins to play with, and aunts and uncles visiting back and forth.

Almost from the day they were born, Anna, Teddy, then Elliot and Corinne, learned Roosevelt traditions. Family tradition meant prayers with Papa in the sitting room every morning, and days filled with lessons, physical exercise, visits, and play. In the evening, the children waited in the library until Papa came home. Then they rushed to greet him, and followed him upstairs to his dressing room. There, they were allowed to watch him shave and change into evening clothes. Even when Mr. and Mrs. Roosevelt dined at home, they always dressed formally for dinner.

Teddy's mother added a special quality to the family's life. As a girl, she had lived on a vast plantation in Georgia. Her family was as important in the South as the Roosevelts were in the North. Martha Roosevelt was an extraordinary person.

Theodore Roosevelt's character was shaped equally by both parents. From his father, he acquired a sense of civic duty and a strict code of honor. Mr. Roosevelt worked hard at his business, but even harder in charitable work. He was one of the organizers of The Children's Aid Society, as well as the Newsboy's Lodging House, which provided beds and meals to stray children. He also was a founder of the New York Orthopedic Hospital, the Metropolitan Museum of Art, and the American Museum of Natural History. In addition, he spent a good deal of time collecting money from friends and associates for other worthwhile charities.

Mrs. Roosevelt was a warm and outgoing woman, always involved with people. She enjoyed telling stories, especially about her heroic ancestors and relations. Teddy loved to hear Mama talk about Grandpa hunting foxes and wildcats; of duels and bear-chases; of brave sailors and daring explorers. The boy dreamed of one day doing brave things himself.

Teddy's dreams seemed to have little chance of coming true. Young Theodore Roosevelt suffered serious attacks of asthma. Each attack made him wheeze and gasp for air. Teddy felt as if he were choking. It was frightening and exhausting. His parents often worried that their small, frail boy would not live to manhood. The attacks came every week or two, without warning, and Teddy was constantly terrified that one might start at any time.

The asthma began in 1862, when Teddy was four years old. The Civil War had erupted the year before, and the whole family was deeply affected by it. The war kept Mr. Roosevelt away

for many months at a time. He had worked out a
plan for Union soldiers to send some of their pay
home each month. That way, their families
would have a small, steady income.

This plan to send home, or allot, part of a soldier's pay had never been done before, and President Lincoln thought it was an excellent idea. He asked Mr. Roosevelt to organize the

project, visit Army camps, and sign up the troops. Mr. Roosevelt spent the rest of the war years at this work, and it was a great success. In fact, the allotment plan became a permanent part of the United States military payroll system.

The Roosevelts were strongly pro-Union during the war. The one exception was Teddy's mother, whose brothers were in the Confederate Navy. In addition, Martha's mother and sister lived with her, and they were also pro-Confederacy. They didn't talk about it in front of the Roosevelt clan, but they acted on it in secret.

Whenever Mr. Roosevelt was away, the three women packaged clothing to be sent to friends in the South. Teddy, his brother, and his sisters didn't really understand what was going on. All they knew was that it was a secret from the other Roosevelts and everyone outside the family. The children liked the idea of a mystery. Yet, they were confused by the divided loyalties in their own home.

Though the war made an impression on the children, it did not change their lives very much. Part of every day was spent with Aunt Anna Bulloch, who tutored all the Roosevelt children. None of them ever attended public schools. This was another family tradition. Aunt Anna taught them reading, writing, and arithmetic. Teddy was terrible at arithmetic, and he continued to dislike it all his life. But reading and writing were always a pleasure for him.

The sickly little boy couldn't do many of the physical things other children did. He was often confined to the house. But he found a way to escape his closed world—by reading. One day he wandered into the family library and opened a large book. The book's title was *Missionary Travels and Researches in South Africa,* by David Livingstone.

Most of the words in the book were too hard for the boy to read, but he found the pictures fascinating. There were zebras, hippopotamuses, elephants, and insects. Teddy

carried the book around for weeks. It was also
the beginning of his lifelong interest in wildlife. Right away, Teddy decided he would be a
naturalist when he grew up, and he would con-
tribute to Papa's American Museum of Natural
History.

Young Theodore Roosevelt planned to learn everything there was to know about nature. Nothing seemed more romantic or exciting than to travel to far-off places, meet all kinds of people, and collect specimens of rare and beautiful plants and animals. But until he could do that, he would find adventure in books. He read natural histories, exciting stories, tales of the American frontier, myths and legends.

Of course, Teddy did not have to spend all of his time indoors, reading. When he was well enough, he played with the other Roosevelt children on the family's back porch, and he was encouraged to run errands around the neighborhood. It was on one of those errands that seven-year-old Teddy saw something that made a deep impression on him. As he later wrote, "I was walking up Broadway, and as I passed the market to which I used sometimes to be sent before breakfast to get strawberries, I suddenly saw a dead seal laid out on a slab of wood. That seal filled me with every possible feeling of romance and adventure."

Teddy came back to see the seal day after day. He looked at it, asked questions about it, measured it up, down, and around. Then he began to write a natural history based on his observations. He wanted to own the animal and display it as a prize specimen. Although Teddy didn't get the whole seal, he was given the skull. With two of his cousins, he promptly started "The Roosevelt Museum of Natural History." The collection's main attraction was the seal skull. Their museum also had field mice, snapping turtles, snakes, and a variety of insects.

Most of Teddy's collecting was done during summer vacations. Every year, the Roosevelt family rented a house in the country. These vacations were special for the Roosevelt children. They were free to run and play outdoors, fish, hike, pick berries, and ride horses. Mr. Roosevelt was a fine horseman, and he made sure the children also had ponies to ride.

Horseback-riding was an activity that Teddy enjoyed all of his life. Many years later, he organized the First United States Volunteer Cavalry Regiment, which was called the Rough Riders. He also bought and worked on two cattle ranches in the Dakota Territory.

In the summer of 1868, when Teddy was nine-and-a-half years old, he began to keep a diary. This was a habit that stayed with him for the rest of his life. In addition, Theodore Roosevelt wrote many books of history, journals about his hunting trips and ranch life, thousands of letters, and a long autobiography.

...this country will not be a permanently good place for any of us to live in unless we make it a reasonably good place for all of us to live in.

The spring of 1869 brought a new experience to Teddy, Anna, Corinne, and Elliot. Their parents took them to Europe. There were a number of reasons for the trip. Mr. and Mrs. Roosevelt felt it would be educational for the children to visit museums, castles, and other historical places. It would be an opportunity to meet important people and to learn some French, German, and Italian language skills. There was another reason for the trip. Mrs. Roosevelt's brothers were living in England. She had not seen them in eight years, since the beginning of the Civil War.

Martha's brothers, Irvine and James Bulloch, had fought for the Confederacy. At the end of the war, they refused to give up their loyalty to the defeated Confederacy. Nor would they swear allegiance to the United States. As a result, they were not allowed to return to America.

For Mrs. Roosevelt, the reunion was joyful.
For Teddy, it was unbelievably exciting. To
him, the Bulloch brothers were dashing military
heroes.

In later years, the grown-up Teddy encouraged James Bulloch to write a book titled *The Secret Service of the Confederate States in Europe.* In turn, Uncle James supplied valuable information for young Roosevelt's own first book, a naval history of the War of 1812. This book was begun when Teddy was a student at Harvard University.

The Roosevelts' trip to Europe lasted a little more than a year. During that time, the family visited England, Scotland, France, Germany, Italy, Austria, and Switzerland. Into Teddy's journal went all kinds of information, especially about nature. One entry, made in France, read: "We saw a tree 1,400 years old. We saw a stream of pure and cold water. We had such a happy time."

Another entry, from France, said: "We went in the park where on a sand bank we made tunnels 10 paces long. After dinner we went to the rocks where we jumped over crevasses and ran in them and had such fun. In one of our rambles we saw very fresh traces of a deer."

It was clear from his writings that eleven-year-old Teddy enjoyed those parts of the trip that were spent outdoors, exploring and playing. The rest of the trip—visiting museums, art galleries, and churches—was less of a pleasure for all of the Roosevelt children.

Mr. and Mrs. Roosevelt had hoped the European tour would be more than educational. They thought it might cure Teddy's asthma. But he had frequent attacks, which continued when the family was back home. Even a summer at Oyster Bay, on New York's Long Island shore and one of the boy's favorite places, made no difference in his health.

Desperate to help the youngster, Mr. and Mrs. Roosevelt considered sending Teddy to the Rocky Mountains, where he might breathe easier. People believed that the thin, dry air in the Rockies was good for asthma sufferers. But the Roosevelts really did not want to send their young boy so far from home, and Teddy did not want to leave his parents and friends.

Mr. and Mrs. Roosevelt decided to try one last remedy—physical activity. Teddy's older sister, Anna, had been born with a back problem. To help her, a doctor recommended body-strengthening exercises. The plan worked.

Because Anna's back had been helped by regular therapy, Mr. and Mrs. Roosevelt hoped the same kind of constant, hard physical exercise might benefit Teddy. One day, Mr. Roosevelt sat down with his son and said, "Theodore, you have the mind, but you have not the body, and without the help of the body the mind cannot go as far as it should. You must *make* your body. It is hard drudgery...but I know you will do it." The boy agreed.

Teddy and his mother began going to Mr. John Wood's Gymnasium every day. Mrs. Roosevelt sat, watched, and encouraged the twelve-year-old boy. He worked with weights— pushing, pulling, and lifting them until he could do no more. He pounded a punching bag, swung dumbbells, and spent hours practicing on horizontal bars. It was drudgery, as his father said it would be, but the boy never complained or allowed himself to stop.

Within a short time, it was clear that the effort was paying off. Week after week passed without an asthma attack. Teddy stayed thin, but his strength grew every day. His arms and legs had a wiry power, even though there were no bulging muscles on them. However, his chest expanded greatly. This was proof to his parents, and to him, that his breathing would continue to get easier.

After three months at Wood's Gymnasium, the Roosevelts set up their own gymnasium and weight equipment on the back porch. Teddy

could work out there as often and as much as he liked. The other Roosevelt children could join him any time they wanted to, and Mrs. Roosevelt didn't have to spend her whole day sitting in the gymnasium.

As Teddy's health improved, he was able to do many more things. During the summer of 1871, he spent an energetic vacation in the Adirondack Mountains of New York State. He

swam in the icy streams and rivers, climbed mountains, went hiking for days, and canoed over swift waters. The boy delighted in a feeling of well-being.

Until now, Teddy had felt that a life of active adventure was out of his reach. Suddenly, such a life *was* possible. Realizing this, the youngster plunged into every activity with great energy and interest. He was enthusiastic about learning everything, and doing everything. It was an enthusiasm that would never leave him.

When Theodore Roosevelt was President and living in the White House, his zest for life often startled people. On winter evenings, he sometimes went swimming in the freezing Potomac River. He built a gymnasium for his children, and used it as much as they did. President Roosevelt also climbed trees, boxed and wrestled with professionals, rode, hunted, and always had a good time. It was as if he was making up for those early years of physical inactivity.

When Teddy was thirteen, he began to look forward to higher education. He wanted to go to Harvard College. To prepare himself, he studied long and hard with tutors in English, German, French, and Latin. Teddy also took lessons in taxidermy from John Bell, the man who had stuffed animals for James Audubon, the famed naturalist.

The boy stuffed every specimen he could acquire, but he soon ran out of animals on which to work. To solve the problem, Mr. Roosevelt gave Teddy a double-barreled shotgun and told him to shoot his own specimens in the woods.

To his dismay, Teddy couldn't hit anything, while his brother and cousins were successful hunters. In fact, Teddy couldn't even see what they were shooting. He told this to his father, and Mr. Roosevelt took Teddy for an eye examination.

In his autobiography, President Roosevelt wrote, "Soon afterwards I got my first pair of spectacles, which literally opened an entirely new world to me. I had no idea how beautiful the world was until I got those spectacles.... I could not see, and yet was wholly ignorant that I was not seeing."

Once he had glasses, young Roosevelt's interests as a naturalist changed. In the past, he had studied mammals—the larger they were, the better. Now he became a bird-watcher, and this interest never left him. As President of the United States, Roosevelt kept a complete list of the birds he saw on the White House grounds. There were fifty-six species on his list.

Theodore Roosevelt's teen years were busy, happy, and educational. He and his family spent a year traveling in Europe and North Africa, and Teddy brought back a fine collection of stuffed birds. Then, in September 1876, when Teddy was almost eighteen, he entered Harvard.

The young Roosevelt stood five feet eight inches, and he was still thin, although the barrel chest of his later years was starting to develop. As a college student, Theodore got excellent marks and was on the boxing and wrestling teams. He also ran track, rowed, and taught Sunday school. He even found time and energy to join several college clubs, to attend concerts, parties and lectures, and to begin work on his first history book.

But the pleasure of those years was diminished when Mr. Roosevelt died, in February 1878. For the rest of his life, Theodore tried to be the fine man his father hoped he would be.

When he was graduated from Harvard with honors, Theodore enrolled at Columbia University Law School, in New York City. After a year, however, a growing interest in politics led the young man to run for the New York State Assembly, an election he won. It was during his third term as assemblyman that Roosevelt suffered a double tragedy. His mother and wife died on the same day. Filled with grief, the young man left politics and went out West.

After two years as a cattleman in the Dakota Territory, Roosevelt came back to New York and resumed his political career. He served on the Civil Service Commission, as New York City's police commissioner, and as Assistant Secretary of the Navy under President William McKinley.

Roosevelt gained national fame in 1898, during the Spanish-American War. As

commander of the Rough Riders, he fought bravely and led his troops well. On his return, he was greeted as a hero, and easily won the election for Governor of New York State.

A year later, Roosevelt ran for Vice President with President McKinley. The McKinley-Roosevelt ticket won, and in March 1901,

Theodore became Vice President of the United States. Six months later, he became President when McKinley was assassinated. Theodore Roosevelt was forty-two years old, the youngest man to become President of the United States.

During his eight years in office, Roosevelt was an active, vigorous President. Under his leadership, the United States government began to conserve the nation's huge natural resources. The number of national parks doubled. Roosevelt's administration also established 16 national monument areas, 51 wildlife refuges, and added 125 million acres to the national forests.

His involvement in foreign policy was equally vigorous. Roosevelt believed that the United States, as a strong, young country, should be an important world power. For example, President Roosevelt declared that the United States would actively protect Latin America against any interference from Europe.

President Roosevelt believed that the United States should use its prestige and power to help maintain world peace. An outstanding example of this came in 1905, during the war between Russia and Japan. Roosevelt offered his services as mediator, a person who tries to settle the differences between two conflicting parties. Roosevelt succeeded in bringing about the war's end. For this, he was awarded the Nobel Peace Prize.

When Roosevelt left the Presidency, in 1909, he intended to enjoy the rest of his life hunting, collecting specimens for museums, and maintaining an active, productive life. He traveled to Africa and South America, wrote a number of books, and led the American Historical Society. But he could not resist a return to politics. In 1912, he ran for President as an independent candidate, but was defeated.

Until his death, on January 6, 1919, Theodore Roosevelt continued to give freely of his time and talents to the America he loved. He left behind a treasury of writings, political accomplishments, a widespread system of parks and forests, and a reputation as a man of honor, courage, and vision.